musings

Rivka Rothstein

BookLeaf Publishing

India | USA | UK

Presentation by *BookLeaf Publishing*

Web: www.bookleafpub.com

E-mail: info@bookleafpub.com

ISBN : 9789357448659

First edition 2021

ACKNOWLEDGEMENT

I would like to acknowledge God. May I ever strive to receive Wisdom and live in Love.

I would also like to thank my wonderfully loving, supportive, and patient parents, Steve and DeeAnn, who have been there for me at each step of the way. And to each and every person I have ever encountered - from deep relationships to fleeting moments - thank you for teaching me more about how to Love.

PREFACE

These poems are the products of various "time outs" from life throughout the past five years. A number of them were written during an extended "time out" where my only tasks each day (apart from healing) were to do yoga, meditate, and write poetry. I wrote each morning and evening directly after meditating with the intention of writing in an unedited stream of consciousness. Most of the poems in this collection are still in their original, unedited format.

time out

traffic marks the point.
the trusty grated nonsense blurring
granted,
we strive and search
without cease
the fires of the engines
flaming with impassioned opinion
virtue falling to second
the babble, a roar
deafening to all who drive
but a quiet exit
with scarcely a note
brings respite

you wait it out
eating your sandwich on the banks of the river

windows

hush the formal flowers of dawn
they swing so sweetly
against the grain
wiping the trails of starlight
from the oaken hewn sky of time

the simple blunder of time
creating the rocky waves
laden with doubt
and shivering, crying for warmth.

oh sands of sadness
wash away my pain
my counterbalance widow begs, screaming

blue-struck, she falters
ripping
her hands lift gently from the sharp rocky shore
blood marked and cut
to bring notice to her wounds

she lifts her eyes and gazes upwards
expectant, surprised, in wonder
and alive

mistified

mistified
the hollow wears a cloak
of soft fabric
a velvet veil of stardust
settled
hovering amidst earthly form
hush
a whisper carries
brilliantly through the fog
time is here
we are now
we have begun

God

treasure the epiphanies
in marvelous wonders
of minuscule
and infinite
proportions

one and the same

the stars rest gently downwards
heralding what is to come
they drench the incandescent fireflies
of earth
and partner with the little guys
one and the same they are
truly noting their humility
their longing for peace
gravity pulling us all along
sure-fire tendencies of chained reactions
we throttle our bottled pride
to listen

chicago

the fall comes late here
as i sit with pricks of insecurities
salting my thoughts too sharply.
the taste (its potency) blazes over the spice of
life
and numbs reception to all other flavor.
God, ease the sting, the insufficient love
i lack the strength myself to cleanse.
seed deep the power i've come to know and trust
let me not blast past for fear of pain
for fear of past becoming present once again
let me taste each subtle, blooming aspect
      in all its glory for what it is
and abstain from how i salt life
with my human hands

i have no name

when heart is lost the home
strays gone.
wandering the moors,
the gray-skies, heathers and streams
leading somewheres...
they may lead home.
but.
the stars. they stray, too.
their courses blanketed by clouds
and the wind hushes gently
leaving the wanderer
penniless
save for the heart
and the chance of the somewhere stream.

sheath

i want
that you tread softly
through my mind body soul
that you breathe my
heartbeat
and cup my
pulse between your hands
like water
from the fountain
that you rim my
edges and
trace my shadow
pursuing the
echo of laughter
in my eyes tears and ghost
i want
that you peer into the pools
of starlit corners
and light the lamp
on the left side
find the room
explore its depths
make its possibilities
concrete in your being

earth

shaded greens whisper gradually
tongues of silhouetted daylight
crouch like gossiping maids and cronies
beneath the gentle foliage
i bend to test the smell of earth
dewy, musty, fertile
crops of moss and mushrooms adorn the forest
floor
the birds begin to sing

and i am home

untitled in tblisi

one of the holies
is kisses of breeze between my fingertips
when embraces of my palm
dance across and whisper
their secrets
to the creases of my history

rainwashed

i am
addict to the electrics of
thunderstorm cleansing

when all control gives way
and impulse
heartbeat
hot, thick blood
reigns on high
with zero nod to
decency

out the window
leaping
careening
if only I could fly
and render myself to the
storm
then I would burst
and shatter
into a million brilliant
daggers of
bliss

wrought iron

time seems drawn
his face lined with
impending
he breaks the light
clenching tightly to the
known increments
the necessary actions
of the confines of the clock

expansion

shred the baseboards the walls the ceiling tiles
make way for the Light
to shine through
to shine free
only the air persisting between Life and
the arms open wide
to embrace with laughter
this beautiful comfort

the present

shaded lilies
roam the valleys decked
with gold
pouring from the sky
the sun surprising the earth
with her gentle caress
an awakening.
smiling,
she stoops to collect
the daisies
and treasure them
next to her lips
'marvelous,'
she whispers,
eyes closed
heart singing the fruits of bliss

our stories

softly guiding waves
break free of wrath
of shame of absence of terror
we share the fabrics of time of tapestries
the sun-soaked wings of shimmering starlight
gratefully beaming down to reach
the grandmothers
the latent bodies of history

we gather here to learn to become
we shatter timbers
we dress the Truth to undress and gaze
upon its beauty

remembrance

gently softly fixed
we cry
stagnant in our offering
the way is blocked
is fogged over by insert what you will

trigger release
remembrance
the gaze of Light into
disheveled corners where any which way
seems fine i'm sure it's fine
i'm sure it's --
crooked based on insert what you will.

again remembrance.
again the fog.
again pain suffering disjointed separation
again remembrance
that we are all that is we are one
and I Am Love and i am whole
in your eyes
a sentient being
callused by the nature of creation
blessed in the nature of creation

perfect in the nature of creation
that is our will of remembrance
to receive the Grace that is our breath
our footsteps forward in time,
the great expanse,
the great cost of living
the great gift of once again
and once again
and once again
remembrance...

whispers of the
water

waded
to wait
wayward we fly
past tall buildings of water
of living light
we know them
feel them
are them
but do not know them
as our own

we turn obligatory circles
whispers reach us
and we learn

before the dawn

grace
traverse the halls

marbled and stony
white lit and honest
not a speck of dust
        caught
the air only light
        the light only pure
the gentlest of blatant honesty

you bow before yourself
        loved for all
lit for all you are worth
peace and surrender
        to God, Your Self

hallowed

there is a lingering
ghost to whispered touch.
seconds later,
the shadow keeps its place
reminding the
skin
of past embraces.
remembering the presence
of something out of air
that brims,
kisses,
and continues
on.

like glances
between two strangers
meant to partner
in the god-given moment.

just for this

timeless, we gather round
anticipation amped to
fighting levels with greed
we toast to shades
of days gone by
to the torrent
that is to come
sweeping us off our feet
to gently put us back down again
reaching up to dust the lips
of inevitability
we are human, you say
fear not.

that which blooms

my tongue the guide
of what cannot be spoken
take away the bonds of time
and revel in that which blooms
crooning magnificence
taken with song
my heart smiling
and when eyes open
i try to remember the infinite
the confines restrict
and i fall away

into the someday of bliss

where i already am